/'po.no/, ['pono] Noun: Hawaiian, do what is right

Do the right thing for your young puppy!

Workbook Guide to Your Puppy's First 4 Months

Developed by Canine Behaviorist, Trainer and Breeder
Deanna Meyer BA Psych, MA Teaching

Your step-by-step guide to shaping your young puppy's manners and behaviors.

Developed by a professional trainer and Labrador Retriever Breeder on the island of Maui, Pono Puppy Method follows the Hawaiian custom of doing the right thing, in this case, for your puppy and your family. Founded on patience, positive reinforcement, and understanding, you will learn how to communicate effectively and listen patiently to what your puppy is telling you. This method is designed to be simple and easy to implement on a daily basis, ensuring that you can truly enjoy your puppy raising journey!

Deanna Meyer BA Psych., MA Teaching, Canine Behaviorist, AKC Certified
Evaluator, AKC Labrador Retriever Breeder

Welcome!

What Makes Pono Puppy Method Unique?

/'po.no/, ['pono] Noun: Hawaiian, do what is right

In order to do what is right for you new puppy, you must begin now! This method captures the moldability of the young puppy. Think of him as a pliable lump of clay, ready to be shaped. The longer you wait to begin shaping his behavior, the harder it will be. Soon, he will become more like a hardened stone, and it will take a metaphorical hammer a chisel to accomplish what you can currently do easily by hand.

Pono Puppy Method focuses heavily on:
- enrichment through **novelty**
- socialization through exposure and **stressors**
- development of appropriate behaviors through **capturing**

This method does not focus on obedience training or operant conditioning, but rather prepares your puppy for that all-important future training. You will learn how to reinforce behaviors and manners that you agree with while extinguishing those you don't. Learn the most effective ways to communicate and reward your puppy, gently and purposefully. Pono Puppy Method will suggest the cues that are most important to introduce to your puppy so that you can research and train those tasks separately.

Read the entire workbook in advance. Then follow along, week by week, as your puppy matures. If your puppy is older than 8 weeks when you begin, combine the weeks you missed to catch up.   For best results, do not skip any sections.

Introduction

Dogs are an altricial species, meaning that puppies are born into this world blind, deaf, and completely helpless. They rely on mama for everything, even relieving themselves! A good mama dog sees to their every need for the first few weeks.

Once puppies open their eyes, begin to hear and start toddling, they also become more vocal and start making their needs known by means of fussing, barking, whining, climbing, and pestering mama.

These behaviors are normal and necessary in order to communicate their needs.

Puppies continue this pattern of behavior throughout puppyhood. Behaviors like biting, mouthing, jumping up, climbing, clamoring, and vocalizing are apparent all through the puppy stages of development. These behaviors are not wrong, or even inappropriate! The issues lie in the fact that humans find these behaviors less than desirable and downright annoying. The most common "problems" new owners express with their puppies are usually all of these very normal behaviors. Humans put very high expectations on pets. This is certainly not wrong, and puppies need help learning to be good family members. Understanding why your puppy behaves as he does is the first step in establishing communication and respect.

When you realize that it is the human who has the higher expectations, it is much easier to be patient and consistent when shaping your new puppy's behaviors. *There is no such thing as a bad puppy!* Will he try to chew on things that don't belong to him? Absolutely, but it's not wrong. Will he jump up on you for attention? Absolutely, but it's not wrong. Will he cry when you crate train him? Absolutely, but it's not wrong. Dogs are not even capable of "right" or "wrong" since they don't rely on a moral code. They simply exist in the moment and rely on instinct and response to their environment. Once we eliminate "right or wrong" from the equation, we can simply focus on helping puppy to adapt to your new expectations. It will also make your puppy raising journey positive and rewarding for you both.

THERE IS NO SUCH THING AS A BAD PUPPY!

Patience and consistency are vital for this process. Your puppy will respond and learn more quickly with calm, patient leadership. Dogs have very little understanding of frustration and impatience. Their best interpretation of frustration is weakness and unreliability. Yes, you will get frustrated at times. But you are a grown-up human and should not share that emotion with your puppy. Keep your frustration and disappointment to yourself. If your puppy is not responding to your expectations, check yourself and see where you can improve upon your communication skills.

Using Stressors

There is a psychological phenomenon called an **extinction burst**. If you have never seen one, it can be a bit disconcerting. For some puppy owners, it can be upsetting and downright scary! In a nutshell, it is simply the puppy's last-ditch effort to avoid doing something he may initially be fearful or apprehensive about. It is firmly imprinted in his DNA as a survival mechanism. It is not to be interpreted as disobedience or defiance. He will throw the toddler-equivalent of a tantrum. He may howl, bark, try to hide, or otherwise try to convey to anyone interested that he thinks he is about to die.

You will learn how to expose your puppy to situations that will most assuredly elicit this response. What could you possibly ask of a puppy to put him in such a state? And why on earth would you do that to your innocent, sweet baby?

The reason is simple. **Growth cannot occur without stress**. Naturally, we would never stress our puppy with anything dangerous or completely overwhelming, but the appropriate amount of stress in the appropriately controlled scenarios will help your puppy learn very valuable self-soothing and stress-coping skills. Pono Puppy Method relies heavily on structured, deliberate, controlled stressors to guide the puppy into using his intrinsic mechanisms for dealing with stressful situations. Most people have witnessed puppies and even older dogs who are frightened and nervous about everything! They become reactive towards other dogs, cower at the vet, and even resort to biting. The root of effective socialization lies in ensuring that the puppy learns to use effective coping skills. A firm understanding and acceptance of using stressors will be important as you complete this course.

It is imperative that we introduce real-life, organic stressors into your puppy's world. Some examples are crate training, separation training, noise desensitization, dog distractions and introductions, grooming, teaching him to swim, nail trimming, and impulse control, just to name a few. The most difficult part of putting your puppy through any process that elicits a potential stress response is that it will definitely tug at the heart strings! In fact, many puppy owners give up at the first sign that their baby might be unhappy with the situation. It is perfectly understandable. However, following through with the process is absolutely vital to his success and growth. Giving up is counterproductive to your goal and will actually reward him for failing. When you follow through, both you and your puppy can celebrate a huge milestone! You will both experience pride and confidence, enough to get you through the next situation, and the next, and the next.

**GROWTH
CANNOT
OCCUR
WITHOUT
STRESS**

In the case of crate training, for example, he will most likely bark, whine, fuss, dig at the door, and become very dramatic about his confinement. Remember that he will do everything he can think of instinctively as a last-ditch effort to stay alive!

This is where most puppy owners give up. It is just too difficult and emotional for the human. Your fear that it is too stressful for the puppy or that you are being cruel to him prevents you from following through. Be assured that you are not being cruel. After all, YOU made the decision to crate train him, and for very good reasons which will be addressed in the crate training section. Be confident that you have made the right decision and stand strong in that. Puppy will try to convince you otherwise and will do his best to get out of having to figure out how to deal with stress. But once he gets through his extinction burst, he will find his built-in coping skills and will settle down. This is an intrinsic reward that he has given himself. It simply feels better. He will start to realize that the best way out of a stressful situation is to use another coping skill like yawning, shaking off, stretching, or nose-licking to help soothe himself, eventually leading to nap time.

If you give up while he is throwing a tantrum, you will reinforce his instinct and he will remain in a fearful state which is counter-productive for development. Don't be tempted to second guess yourself. Be sure that everyone in the house understands what an extinction burst is and are prepared to ride it out as it will be noisy for a while! Giving up because it is too stressful for YOU is absolutely not an option. This workbook will prepare you and should give you the confidence you need to follow through.

DON'T GIVE UP
DON'T GIVE IN

Remember that stress is absolutely necessary for growth. In the wild stress occurs naturally and the puppies who learn how to cope will thrive. Our domesticated pups must learn through contrived stress which, thankfully, we can control. Too many puppies/dogs have been sheltered, coddled, and protected from appropriate stressors, resulting in behaviors that are difficult to counter-condition later in life. Resolve now to put in the time, energy, and patience to shape your puppy into the well-balanced, confident dog he is meant to be.

Contents

WEEK 13
- Sit and Down on Cue
- Off Switch
- What If...

WEEK 14
- Wants vs. Needs
- Advanced Impulse Control
- Time-Outs

WEEK 15
- Advanced Leash Skills
- Equipment
- Balance

WEEK 16
- Preparing for Outings
- Expectations
- Managing Greetings
- Leadership
- Building Focus

Week 8

Everything is bliss right now! Your puppy will sleep, and sleep, and sleep...a lot! This is necessary and vital to his growth and development. But when he is awake, make the most of that precious time.

Capturing Behaviors

Introducing your puppy to new ways to ask for things is an example of capturing behaviors. It is one of the most effective, non-verbal, and long-lasting ways for him to learn. Puppies do things that we like all the time! They also do things we are not so fond of. It is your job to teach puppy how you expect him to act in your household. The more you can help shape the puppy's behaviors by rewarding the things you like and redirecting or ignoring the behaviors you don't, the faster and easier he will learn. Not only does the puppy learn more effectively, but the human stays calmer and more engaged with the pup. Non-verbal training helps both ends of the leash to stay relaxed, consistent and patient.

Marking

Marking is a way of communicating to the puppy instantly that you like what he is doing. Offering him a treat when he does well is great, but it can take too long for him to make the correlation since it can take several seconds to get the treat in his mouth. Yes, he will lose focus in that amount of time! Once he is loaded to a marker (described below) you will have a faster, more effective tool for shaping his behavior. Choose whether you would prefer a verbal marker or a clicker. The downside to using a verbal marker is that our emotions can come through at times. If puppy does extremely well, we may be tempted to use a more enthusiastic "YES!!!" rather than a consistent tone of voice. A clicker, however, is consistent and always sounds the same, so it is very clear to the puppy as to its meaning. If you opt for a verbal marker, be consistent and be sure that everyone in the household can, as well.

Loading to a Marker

Sit on the floor with puppy. Have your treat pouch ready with good value treats. If you are using a verbal marker, say "yes" in a tone that you will use every time for marking, then deliver the treat immediately. If you are using a clicker, same sequence applies, "click"/treat. Repeat the sequence for 20 repetitions. Wait for puppy to get organically distracted. He will be engaged with you for a bit since you have treats, so give him enough time to distract himself. When he does, mark him with your verbal marker or clicker. If he is loaded, he will look at you. If he does not respond, repeat the sequence several more times until he responds when distracted.

Using a Marker

In the manners example, you are simply watching puppy and waiting for him to sit down. As soon as that bottom touches the floor, mark with "yes" or click, and deliver the treat. After a few repetitions, move around a bit so you can practice again. He will need to be standing before you expect him to volunteer a sit. Tease him with the treat a bit so he gets a bit excited, then wait for the sit. When he does, mark and treat. This works for any behavior you want to capture. This is not operant conditioning. Do not use a verbal cue or hand signal of any kind. Simply wait, and reward. If he does not volunteer the behavior you are looking for, he simply does not get the reward. This takes patience on your end. Do not rush and do not worry if he does not comply at times. He will catch on quickly if you give him a chance.

Behaviors To Capture at This Age

Most of your capturing will be when your puppy makes a choice to hold back and use his first experience with impulse control; when he makes the choice to keep his feet on the floor instead of jumping up, when he decides to remain quiet and wait patiently for the toy instead of barking, when he settles down as you hold him instead of struggling, or when he allows you to take something from him instead of running away with it.

CAPTURING IS NOT CUEING!
SEE THE BEHAVIOR
MARK THE BEHAVIOR
TREAT THE BEHAVIOR

REMAIN NON-VERBAL

HOMEWORK

CLICKER TRAINING RESEARCH

Extra-curricular homework: research different types of clicker training and marking of behaviors. It is not necessary to use a clicker if you can be consistent with a verbal marker.

Having a good understanding of marking behaviors will help you reward your puppy quickly and effectively for desired behaviors. You do not need to become a dog psychologist to become adept in marking behaviors. It is simple and effective and a great communication tool that you can use for life.

Manners

This is the first thing you will teach your puppy in terms of capturing behaviors. The best way to teach your puppy to use his manners is to simply capture the behavior when it happens. In this way, you are teaching puppy that he gets what he wants by volunteering a behavior that you find appropriate. Your idea of manners may differ from someone else's, so decide what behavior you are looking for and be ready to reward it. For most people, that behavior looks like a 'sit'. After all, if he is sitting, he can't be doing another annoying behavior like jumping up. If you have a particularly bouncy puppy, you might decide that just keeping all four feet on the floor is manners enough.

Once you have decided what good manners looks like, it's time to show him that using those manners pays off.

Start by tempting him with energy, a toy, or a treat. In his excitement, he will use his puppy language to express his interest. Most likely this will include jumping up, mouthing or biting, or barking. This is the fun part! You don't have to do anything but wait! Sounds easy, but when you put it into practice you will be surprised how difficult it is to resist the urge to "make" your puppy sit. This is not operant conditioning, so do not tell or show him what to do. Simply wait and withhold the item he is interested in. When his antics fail, he will get confused or bored and will sit as a natural response. This is what you are waiting for! Immediately mark him with your marker ("yes!" or click) and deliver the treat. Give enough praise that he is rewarded, then start again.

It will take him several repetitions to figure out that his behaviors have a direct correlation to the reward. He will certainly make some mistakes over the next few trials, but that is good because he is figuring out what *doesn't* work and that there is only one correct answer; sit. This is a non-verbal game and should always be played silently, short of a marker word and praise. Do not give the puppy any correction or instruction. The goal is that he figures out the answer for himself. The most difficult part of this game is the human's patience level. Just stay calm, relaxed, and consistent and puppy will learn. This game sets the stage for more advanced impulse control later, so it is a perfect place to start. If your puppy's breeder used Pono Puppy Method, he will automatically use his manners by 8 weeks of age. If not, he will pick it up quickly.

CAPTURING MANNERS

TEASE WITH TOY OR TREAT
PAUSE AND WAIT!
WAIT SOME MORE!
IGNORE THE JUMPING
IGNORE THE BITING
TRUST THE PROCESS
MARK AND TREAT THE SIT

The Manners Pact

Young puppies learn very quickly and what they learn sticks with them. However, you can inadvertently counter condition all of that learning by rewarding poor manners absentmindedly. That means that once you teach your puppy how to speak politely, you must insist that he do so always.

ONLY REWARD GOOD MANNERS!

MINDFULNESS MATTERS

Instruct everyone who lives with the puppy to avoid any type of reward when puppy is being very demanding or has forgotten to use his manners. If he jumps up for attention and is rewarded, even once in a while, it will confuse him, and he will be more likely to fail more often. Reward good manners with affection, attention, and plenty of praise. Be patient. He is developing his impulse control and it takes time and maturity.

Crate Training and Potty Training

Crate training is a key component in helping your puppy learn impulse control, self-soothing skills, and for keeping him and his surroundings safe. Dogs instinctively like and seek a den-like place to sleep. It is not cruel to use a crate and it should never be used as punishment. Similar to your bedroom and comfortable bed, it is a place that your puppy will associate with peace, quiet, rest, and safety. It is also a big help in potty training. Create a pleasant space complete with bedding, a few toys, and a water dish that attaches to the side to prevent spilling. Consider your climate and offer a heating or cooling source if necessary.

Be sure your puppy's crate is the appropriate size for his breed. Remember that larger breeds grow very quickly so choose a size that he will fit through his first year. Larger crates often come with a divider which can be used while puppy is small. The space should be just large enough for him to stand, turn around, and sleep. If it is too big, he may soil it.

Begin crate training the first day you bring your puppy home. Ideally, your puppy will sleep in his crate right next to your bed. This way, he can hear and smell you and you can hear him when he needs to go potty at night. This is where the potty training begins. Puppies generally do not want to soil their sleeping and eating areas. Since his crate is only big enough for sleeping at this age, he will fuss when he needs to relieve himself. This is the first step in teaching him that he must tell you when he needs to go outside. Do not wake him up to go potty at night. Let him wake you up instead. After all, he may be able to hold it longer than you think! Part of potty training is actually potty "holding". He will learn to "hold it" until you can get him outside to his potty spot.

Make sure your puppy is set up for a good first night. He should be ready to settle in for the night if he has had enough exercise, proper feeding times, has gone potty, the temperature is comfortable for him, and his space is cozy, quiet, and dark. It is helpful to have 2 crates; one for nighttime, next to your bed, and another in the common space in the house where he can be confined for naps but amidst the activity of the home. An ideal setup includes and exercise pen, which is a larger confined space where your puppy can play, eat, sleep, and have a bit more freedom until he is ready to earn more privileges in the home.

CRATE TRAINING SUCCESSFULLY

- **CORRECT SIZE CRATE**
- **GOOD TEMPERATURE CONTROL**
- **SPILLPROOF WATER DISH**
- **CHEW TOYS FOR BOREDOM**
- **APPROPRIATE BEDDING**
- **PUPPY APPROPRIATELY FED AND RELIEVED**
- **PUPPY TIRED AND READY FOR SLEEP**

When you cannot be watching him, he should be in his exercise pen or crate so that he does not have accidents. Take him outside regularly. If he has been playing hard and after naps, he will most definitely need to go outside. The key to potty training is to be on a schedule and to be watchful of his behaviors. He will move away from his play area and may look a bit panicky. Pick him up quickly and take him to his relieving area. Praise him and let him play a little outside before bringing him back inside. If he has an accident, oh well! Clean it up and be more watchful next time. Avoid punishment for accidents. He may become fearful of going potty in front of you, which will complicate your training process.

You will most likely encounter that dreaded extinction burst your first night of crate training. For most puppies, this is the first time he has been alone to sleep, and it can be strange and confusing. You do not need to offer him any consolation or pity. The only thing you can do for him is to wait it out. He will figure out how to soothe himself eventually. Hang in there! It won't last forever. Accepting that it is normal and expected should help. Resolve to follow through, no matter what. The skills he learns from crate training last his entire life. Putting the time in now will pay off exponentially in the long run.

Be consistent with crate time. Ideally, he will learn to nap several times a day in his crate, as well as overnight. This is his safe, quiet, peaceful place. You can expect that he will come to love and seek it when he needs to be alone and quiet. For some puppies who can't quite shut down on their own, it is a valuable tool for helping him learn his "off switch". In addition, every puppy will need to visit the vet at some point. Occasionally, they may need to spend the day or even overnight at the clinic. Crate trained puppies fare much better than puppies who are nervous or fearful of being confined. If you ever plan to board him, most facilities require the dog to be crate trained for his comfort.

Daytime Potty Training

Potty training at night is relatively easy since he is close to you and in his crate. This helps him begin to understand that YOU are part of the potty equation. He must get your attention when he needs to "go".

During the day, it is much easier to lose track of him and much easier for him to forget to ask you. The remedy is attention. If you cannot see him and he wanders off, he will have an accident. It is easier for him to find his own favorite spot than to come and find you. This is another reason why the exercise pen is a great tool. Keep him in the pen or crate when you cannot watch him.

When to take him outside

Puppies have a fairly predictable schedule for relieving. Pay attention to his habits and take note of when he seems to need to potty regularly. Some general rules are:

- upon waking from nighttime or naps
- after eating
- after high-energy playtime
- when experiencing stress, which you will be introducing in this method.

Watch for these behaviors and be ready to get him to his potty spot quickly:
- sniffing around, away from his playing area
- running to the door where he normally goes outside
- wandering off
- circling/spinning

Potty Training Schedule

MON	TUES	WED	THURS	FRI	SAT	SUN
TIME #1/#2	TIME #1/#2	TIME #1/#2	TIME #1/#2	TIME #1/#2	TIME #1/#2	TIME #1/#2

Novelty:
Introducing Stressors

Effective socialization means exposing the puppy to all types of novelty. But that is just the beginning. What is important is how he is feeling about any particular situation. Shy puppies need more time to adjust to new things. Be patient and let him decide for himself when he is ready to investigate. Watch for signs of curiosity and bravery and only reward that state of mind. Never force a puppy into a situation that is too overwhelming for him. Keep novelty simple and safe.

Encourage him when he shows that he in interested and seeking enrichment. It is less common to experience extinction burst during novelty exposure since the situations and novelty items are usually less stressful for the puppy. Using novelty is gently introducing stressors to the puppy. The simple fact that he has never had this experience before constitutes a stressor. The importance of controlling the novelty is that you also control the stressor. Ideas for novelty follow in later paragraphs.

Novelty Guidelines

Keep the item or situation safe and fun. ***Never introduce something to the puppy that you cannot control.*** If you are unsure about a person, animal, situation, or item, exclude it from your list of possible novelty items.

If your puppy shows fear, which is addressed below, use proximity and intensity control to adjust to your puppy's temperament. That means move the stimuli further away and keep sounds and movements lower and slower until he begins to accept it. Introducing novelty should be fun, creative, and rewarding for you and your puppy.

NOVELTY IS THE CORE OF YOUNG PUPPY SOCIALIZATION

How to Handle Fear

Be sure to give him enough space that he can still experience the novelty but is not overwhelmed by it. Sit with him and be as neutral as possible. Do not hold or coddle him or try to "help" him feel better! It is not possible. If you feel sorry for him or try to comfort him, he will not tap into his own coping skills, which is what we are trying to develop. Instead, be his anchor.

This process is not about you. It is about developing his natural coping responses. Give him the time and space he needs to find his own coping skills so that he learns how to calm himself and deal with stressors. It is very tempting to try to soothe the puppy. Dogs interpret coddling and pity as weakness and a lack of confidence. Dogs do not soothe each other. They model curiosity (or fear) and provide silent confidence and support for each other.

It is also tempting to remove the stressor, like letting him out of the crate while he's crying, if you think your puppy is afraid. But remember that the stressor you introduced is completely safe and enriching or you wouldn't have introduced it. If you are not overwhelming him or causing him harm, you can be confident in your approach. Nothing you introduce to him in this method will be harmful or negative, so rest confidently in your approach. The reward will be watching his confidence grow.

**NEVER
CODDLE A
FEAR
RESPONSE**

Gaining Confidence

After a fear response, evidence of him starting to use his coping skills will be apparent when he becomes more curious, sniffing toward the novelty or even moving towards it, and generally relaxing. He may start doing something else like sniffing around or scratching an itch. If he was overly fearful initially, the stress signals will diminish, and he will have an overall more relaxed body language. He may give a big shake off, like when he's wet. As soon as you see him begin to cope on his own, you can offer him treats and affection. Support his decision to give curiosity a try! Until now, you have been his silent anchor. Now is the time to show him that you agree with his bravery and enrichment seeking. He may even get brave enough to interact with the item, which will provide intrinsic rewards and boost his confidence even further.

Your overall goal of introducing novelty and stressors is to build his confidence. Confident dogs have fewer behavioral issues, are calmer, and generally easier to live with than shier, under socialized dogs. Choose novelty and stressors that will be true-to-life in your world.

Novelty At Home

Introduce him to something novel every day this week. It can be a new person, an animal, a bouquet of balloons, blow bubbles for him, wear hats around the house, or even just a large cardboard box! Get creative and have fun! If it is new to him, it counts. Play some loud sounds and determine his reaction. If he is fearful, play the sound more quietly as you feed him treats. Try animal sounds, traffic, and children. Bring as much fun and gentle stimulation as possible into his world. Remember to be mindful of his state of mind and how he is feeling about each new situation and adjust by using proximity and intensity. If the sounds are too loud, turn down the volume. If the item is too large or moves too much, keep it further from him until he shows more curiosity.

Novelty in the World

Start by getting him comfortable in the car. The best place for puppy is in a crate. If your car cannot accommodate, the backseat or far back of a van or SUV will suffice. There are specially made harnesses with a safety belt to secure puppy for a safe journey. A regular harness and leash tethered to a secure point will work, too. At no time should puppy be allowed to roam freely around the car or sit on the driver's lap. This is incredibly dangerous. Once you decide the best place for your puppy to ride, be consistent and ask him to ride there every trip. Watch for signs of sickness or anxiety. If he has never traveled, he may be nervous for the first few trips, or even get car sick. Take short rides initially so he doesn't get overwhelmed. Make sure he is already tired so he will learn to enjoy being rocked to sleep.

Once he is comfortable in the car, try a visit to a big box hardware store that is pet friendly. Carry him through the parking lot and let him ride in the cart inside the store. Bring a blanket or mat so that he is comfortable. Since he can't make the decision to get away from a human or anything else that may frighten him, be very watchful of his body language. If he cowers or looks away from people as they try to pet him, do not allow the greeting and give him space. Bring treats and let strangers offer him one. Be sure to tell them to pet him under the chin so strangers aren't reaching over his head, which some dogs do not appreciate.

Keep some disinfecting wipes in your car and wipe him and his feet down after your outing. At your discretion, visit other places that are not heavily dog trafficked; trips to family or friends' homes, rides in the car, being carried on a hike, or pushed in a dog stroller around the neighborhood are all relatively safe outings for your young pup. Assess the risks for yourself so you are comfortable and confident in your approach to this early exposure to the world. Be sure to have a conversation with your veterinarian about the risks of Parvo and how to take caution out in the world. If you are not comfortable taking him into the world yet omit this portion of the method. You can make up for some novelty at home.

Pono Puppy Method does not endorse or encourage taking unvaccinated puppies anyplace that could pose a risk to his health. Avoid dog parks, beaches, parks, hikes, greeting dogs you do not know, overly stimulating venues like concerts, fairs, and even farmer's markets, especially if your puppy is on the shy side. Use the worksheet to brainstorm places that you can safely and productively take puppy.

Fear Response to Novelty

Ideally, your puppy will become curious and interested in new things. But every puppy will show signs of fear or apprehension at times. Some puppies are particularly shy by nature due to poor breeding, under-socialization by the breeder, or trauma in the neo-natal stage. As you get to know your puppy's temperament, you will be able to adjust the level of novelty accordingly.

Signs that he is anxious may include:
- tail tucked tightly
- cowering down
- hiding behind you
- shaking
- sitting with one paw lifted
- trying to hide or get away
- yelping
- showing other stress signals like excessive yawning or shaking off

Research Assignment

Do an online search of "Dog Stress Signals". On the following page, make a list of **at least 5 behaviors** that signal stress in the puppy. Then, follow the chart on the next page to track if your puppy shows any of the behaviors in response to the stressors listed. If he does show stress, jot down what you did to help him use his coping skills.
- giving him more **distance**,
- decreasing the stressor's **intensity**,
- giving him **time** to think.

DOG STRESS SIGNALS

VISIBLE BEHAVIORS

DOG STRESS SIGNALS WORKSHEET

RECORD YOUR PUPPY'S RESPONSE IN TERMS OF STRESS SIGNALS AND WHAT ADAPTATIONS YOU USED TO HELP HIM COPE AND GAIN CONFIDENCE.

Type of Novelty Stressor	PUPPY STRESS SIGNALS	CHANGED *DISTANCE* DECREASED *INTENSITY* GAVE MORE *TIME*
CRATE TIME		
NAIL TRIMMING		
INTRODUCTION TO OTHER PETS		
VACUUM CLEANER		
COLLAR AND LEASH		
TEACHING MANNERS		
CAR RIDES		
GROOMING		
BATHING		
PUPPY HANDLING		

DOG STRESS SIGNALS WORKSHEET

Type of Novelty Stressor	PUPPY STRESS SIGNALS	CHANGED *DISTANCE* DECREASED *INTENSITY* GAVE MORE *TIME*
BLOWING BUBBLES		
SKATEBOARD OR BIKE PASSING BY		
MEETING A FRIENDLY STRANGER		
MEETING AN OLDER DOG		
WALKING ON STRANGE SURFACE LIKE BUBBLE WRAP OR FOIL		
RIDING IN SHOPPING CART OR STROLLER		
WATCHING KIDS PLAYING		
WATER PLAY IN BABY POOL		
WATCHING TRAFFIC		
LISTENING TO NEW SOUNDS		

Week 9

Your puppy should be offering manners more reliably by now. He should be settling more quickly in his kennel and napping several times a day still. Now is the time to introduce recall along with establishing boundaries around the house.

Recall

Getting your puppy to come when you call him is the most important thing you can teach him. It is incompatible with other undesirable behaviors like jumping up, running off with items, and much more. If you only teach him one thing, let it be recall.

Start With Chase

Puppies instinctively chase things that move. Remember that Pono Puppy Method relies heavily on capturing behaviors and you can use your puppy's natural chase drive to teach him to come to you on command. Start by playing a little game of "chase me" with him. He chases you, NOT the other way around! Never chase your puppy! When he chases you, it is the foundation for recall. If you chase him, you are sending him away and it is counterproductive to your recall.

As he chases you, adjust your movement so he can "catch" you. When he does, give him plenty of affection and a high value treat. Then walk or jog away and repeat the game. This only takes a few minutes each time you play, so don't overdo it. Keep your sessions short and fun! It's OK if he doesn't engage or want to play your silly game at times. There is nothing at stake and since we are just capturing a behavior that we like, he really can't fail at this point.

If you have a fenced yard or larger space available, you can play this game outside. As he starts to understand that he gets rewarded for coming close to you, make it more difficult by "hiding" partway behind objects, furniture, trees, etc. Remember that you are not cuing him or calling him at this point! Avoid coaxing or calling to him. That will come soon. For now, you are simply waiting for him to voluntarily come close to you and rewarding him. We will put the task on command later.

NEVER CHASE YOUR PUPPY!

Puppies can get very excited during the "chase me" game. This can lead to jumping up and even nipping at clothing and hands. To avoid this, be very watchful and be ready to deliver the reward down low, right on his level. You can have a toy ready, too, to redirect his mouth. Avoid correcting him for the jumping or mouthing and focus on rewarding him for following you. The unnecessary behaviors will fade when he figures out that there is a toy or treat involved. If children are involved in working with the puppy, be sure that they understand and are capable of delivering a reward in a timely manner. If they cannot, stay involved and take charge of the rewards so that the puppy does not practice poor behaviors with the children.

Developing Focus

Getting your puppy's attention and focus can be difficult at times. His attention span is short right now, but it will develop with your guidance as he matures. There are several tools you can use to make this process easier:

- **Backpedaling**
- **Watch Me**
- **Recall**
- **Touch**

BACKPEDALING

If he is having trouble focusing on you during you game of chase, for example, try *backpedaling*. This is just walking or jogging backwards so you are facing him. It is more enticing since he can see your eyes. Eye contact is the foundation of focus skills, so you want him to offer you his eyes often.

WATCH ME

Teaching your puppy to look you in the eyes helps him tune out all other distractions around him. Make a game of watching him in various situations and marking/treating him every time he voluntarily looks at you. Show him that you really like it when he looks at you. See how many times he will look at you in a 3-minute span.

After a few days of capturing this behavior and rewarding it, start putting it on the verbal cue, "*Watch Me*!" Use a happy tone to encourage eye contact. Now you have added a label to his action. He is not ready to respond on cue yet, however. Continue to label his action with "Watch Me!" for the rest of the week.

TOUCH

This task will get your puppy to focus on you and come to you without calling him. The goal is to have him touch his nose to your hand. Obviously, this means he must come very close to you. Start by holding your hand out, palm up, just in front of his nose. He will naturally touch your hand out of curiosity. When he does, mark and treat. This will be an accident the first few times, but soon he will see a pattern. Repeat several times without changing anything. Let him take a break and practice again. As he starts to understand, move your hand into a new position, keeping it easy to reach but a bit further away so that he has to move his feet (come closer to you) in order to touch your hand.

Be sure that you are not moving your hand towards his nose! You already know how to touch his nose, now teach him to touch your hand.

As he gets better at it, you can move your hand to new positions, higher, lower, off to the side, etc. You will use this tool later when you begin outings and leash work. It is an easy, rewarding focus skill.

RECALL ON CUE

Several days into week 9, you can start labeling the action of recall. He should be fairly reliable at following you around and playing your "chase" game for rewards. Now we are going to teach him that his action has a name, and that name is "Come!" You can use any word you choose, but for the sake of simplicity, "come" will be used in this workbook.

There are several steps involved in teaching good recall:

- First, get his attention. Use his name or a sound that ensures that he will look at you.
- Next, start moving away from him as if you are playing your "chase me" game. In a cheery tone, say "Come!" This will trigger him to start to follow you.
- Third, slow down enough so that he can catch you. Be sure you have your treat ready!
- Fourth, lure him very close to you, between your legs using the treat to coax him as close as possible. You should be bending over.
- Next, let him lick and bite at the treat while you pet him around the collar area with the other hand.
- Finally, give the remainder of the treat, stop petting, stand up, and walk away from him.

- **ATTENTION**
- **MOVE!**
- **COAX**
- **LURE HIM UNDER**
- **TREAT AND PET**
- **RELEASE**
- **WALK AWAY**

All of the steps are important. Skipping steps will potentially make your recall weak. Here is why:

- Getting his attention is obvious. If he is not listening, he cannot respond.
- Moving backwards when he looks at you cues him that it is time to play the game you taught him previously, "chase me". Using a fun, happy tone of voice when you say "Come!" will keep the game fun and engaging.
- Having a treat ready and luring him as close as possible prevents you from needing to reach out over his head to touch him or give the treat. All too often, owners only use recall when it is time to leash the puppy or to end whatever fun he was having, thus creating head-shyness and a tendency to take the treat and run off again. Insisting that he come all the way to you and allow himself to be touched and pet around the collar area ensures that he will allow it when it is truly necessary.
- Once he has received his treat and your affection, it is important that YOU are the one to walk away first. It shows him that you are done with him and he is free to go. Most likely, he will actually follow you, solidifying your recall even further.

The Recall Pact

Not only is it vital that you follow every step involved in teaching good recall, but you must also make a pact with your puppy that you will reward every time, you will play it several times daily, and that you will make recall the best game ever! It will be fun, engaging, and positive...every time!

This pact may seem simple initially, but owners have a tendency to stop playing recall as a game and only use it when they really need it, which is generally when it is time for the puppy to come inside, to come away from something that he found very interesting, and to basically end whatever fun the puppy was having. Another tendency humans have is to become frustrated and angry when the puppy starts ignoring the recall game. If you use an angry, threatening tone of voice, your recall will erode. Check yourself and ask, "would I come to me?" If your recall fades, chances are that you have broken your recall pact with your puppy.

Establishing Boundaries

As your puppy matures, he will naturally become more curious and adventurous. Your house is puppy proofed for his safety, and for the safety of your household items, but eventually, he will need to learn to exist in a world full of items that do not belong to him and that he cannot touch. It is your job to establish boundaries and teach him to respect things that belong to the humans.

Leave It

Your puppy has a natural fear response built in for survival. Refer back to the topic of stressors as a reminder how we can take advantage of this response to help us shape behaviors and establish respect and a healthy, normal "fear" for things that do not belong to him.

Be deliberate about introducing forbidden items to your puppy. Start by putting a leash on him and keep ahold of your end. Toss an item on the floor near him, something like a shoe or sock. Be ready! He will most likely dive for it. The leash will be his boundary and he will not be able to get to the item. He will try again several times and fail each time since you are preventing him from succeeding. This is modified capturing. Your job with the leash is to help guide him to the correct answer which is to avoid or ignore the forbidden item.

When he fails several times in a row, he will get a bit confused and stop trying. When he does, mark him and reward! You have just captured him doing the behavior you want, NOT trying to get to the item. Repeat this process with a few other items, rewarding each time he gives up trying.

After a few days of practice, you can add the cue "Leave It!" To be sure that he is truly decided to leave it alone, he needs to voluntarily look at you and not continue to stare at the item. Do not cue him to look at you, simply wait. He will be expecting his reward and will eventually look to you for his treat.

Continue to reinforce respect for human and forbidden items in this manner deliberately with the leash for the remainder of the week. Test him by holding the leash very loosely to determine if he will stop himself just with the "Leave It" cue. Be sure you always reward him by marking and treating for offering the correct response.

Leash Skills

Walking a young puppy on a leash is messy at best! The goal at this age is to simply encourage him to walk with you. You have already introduced this skill with the recall training. Walking on a leash is just a closer version of the "chase game". Reward him the same way by offering a treat and attention every time he comes close to your side.

You will be practicing this in your home and yard so distractions will be fewer than out in the world. He will more than likely bite at the leash, pull back, and even throw himself on the ground and refuse to move! This is all normal puppy nonsense. After all, a leash is a very human invention and puppies find it restrictive and bothersome. Avoid pulling on him or insisting that he walk perfectly at your side. You will just be setting yourselves up for failure. Instead, focus on keeping his attention and playing your "chase game". Keep your sessions short, just a few minutes at a time, several times a day. This is just an introduction the feel of the leash and the concept of walking with you and staying engaged. His attention span is still very limited, so take your time and be patient.

Playtime

Puppies love to play, and they learn all about their world through appropriate playtime. They also need boundaries in their play to establish respect, bite inhibition, and impulse control.

It is ideal to play with your puppy by using toys. Games like fetch, tug, and catch are great fun and we can incorporate lots of fun learning as we play. The "chase game" is great fun for humans and puppies and reinforces your recall and focus skills. Avoid wrestling or playing roughly with your hands. Your puppy will interpret your hand as another puppy and will be more likely to bite and chew on you.

IT IS A PUPPY'S JOB TO BITE. IT IS YOUR JOB TO NOT BE BITTEN

It your puppy puts his mouth on you during playtime, redirect him quickly onto a toy. Puppies bite. That is their favorite means of connection and exploration. It is your job to avoid being bitten! Keep your hands inaccessible to the puppy's mouth as much as possible. Save your touch for grooming, affection, and handling. He will outgrow much of his mouthiness, but until then he needs your help to be successful.

Week 10

By now your puppy is awake more often and ready for more challenges! It's time to make him start to "work" for things in his world and introduce the stressor of impulse control.

Mealtime Manners

Since food is your puppy's greatest resource, you can use it to teach him how to earn all of the wonderful things in his life. He has been figuring out that you appreciate and reward good manners so this should be a fairly easy task for him to learn.

Pick up the puppy's food dish and fill it. The rule is that you control the food, not the puppy. He can do whatever he wants to, but he will not earn his meal until he volunteers good manners, aka, sit.

CONTROL THE FOOD, NOT THE PUPPY

As you lower the bowl to the floor, watch the puppy. If he gets up, raise the bowl back up. If he moved towards you, put him back where he was and repeat the process. It will take him a few tries, but he will soon stop trying to get up and go to the dish.

Once you can set the dish on the floor without him getting up, quickly tell him "OK!" and step back out of the way and allow him to go eat.

It is normal for him to be a bit reluctant to approach the food the first time since he was rewarded for holding back previously. You can give him some encouragement if necessary and move the bowl closer to him if he won't approach. Remember that we are not withholding food from him, we are asking him to use some impulse control and wait to be released before he eats.

Since he eats 2-3 times per day, you have several opportunities to work on this each day. You can even divide each meal into smaller portions and practice a few times at each meal.

Delivering Treats

Puppies are often very excited about receiving treats. There are ways to ensure that your fingers stay intact while you reward your little one.

The key here is that you *deliver* the treat, he does not *take* the treat. There is a big difference! When you deliver the treat, you control it and the manner in which you give it to the puppy. When the puppy is allowed to take it from you, he is in control and will most likely get too excited and not be mindful of his sharp puppy teeth.

The best way to deliver the treat is to hold it in the palm of your hand with a closed fist. In the spirit of capturing the behavior you want, you simply let him lick, paw, nibble at your hand in an attempt to get to the treat. When this fails, he will pull back to think about what to try next. When he does, immediately get the treat into his mouth. Repetition will prove to him that NOT trying to get the treat will actually get him the treat!

When you are delivering a treat as a reward for a behavior, avoid pulling your hand away from his mouth. It is perfectly ok for him to be licking at your hand as you hold the treat. While he is learning the art of taking the treat nicely, he will still make mistakes. If you are quick with your delivery, he will have less of a chance to grab at the treat. If you pull your hand, and thus the treat, up and away from him, you are encouraging him to jump up in order to get it. Keep your hand at his mouth or chest level so he has no need nor desire to try to grab the treat. You know that you are delivering the treat correctly if your hand is slimy!

YOU *DELIVER* TREATS, PUPPY DOES NOT *TAKE* TREATS

If you have a "baby shark" puppy, meaning that he jumps and grabs at the treat, you may need to shape the way he responds to treat rewards. Hold the treat in a closed hand or tightly between your fingers. Let him lick, bite, and paw at your hand. As soon as he STOPS trying to get to the treat, immediately put it in his mouth. This follows the capturing method as you simply wait for him to volunteer a more polite behavior.

Teaching Behaviors on Cue

You have been capturing and rewarding good manners and voluntary behaviors for a few weeks so far. Now you can begin labeling those behaviors and tasks as you begin more communication with your puppy.

You should continue to capture desirable behaviors as your puppy matures, but it is also important and useful to ask the puppy to perform a task on cue. This is the first step in his obedience training. This workbook provides only an introduction to these tasks and a suggestion for which tasks to begin training.
  Do more research and find more resources for training these tasks on cue.

The main behaviors you will put on a verbal cue initially are:
- come/recall (taught on cue previously)
- leave it (taught on cue previously)
- sit
- down
- watch me
- touch

SIT   Since he should be sitting voluntarily by now, it will simply be a matter of labeling the behavior. Tease him a bit with a treat. When he volunteers a sit, say "sit!" and reward him. Repeat this for about 10 repetitions. Then allow him to get organically distracted a bit. Call him back, hold out the treat to the end of his nose and say "sit!" BEFORE he offers it. Repeat again for about 10 repetitions. Test it by allowing him to get distracted again, calling him back, and asking for the sit before he offers it. If he does not sit right away, do NOT repeat the verbal cue! This is important. He will learn to ignore your first cue and will wait for you to repeat yourself. It is also a test in patience on your end. Give him several seconds or longer to figure out what you want from him. It is not necessary at this age for him to plant his bottom immediately. Be patient and fair and kind as he learns.

To teach the down position, ask him to sit first. Hold a food lure right to the end of his nose. He will lick at it and try to get it. That's ok. Hold it so he cannot take it from you. Slowly lower the treat/your hand to the floor. His head will follow. As his head gets lower to the floor, it will be more comfortable for him to move into a down position. As soon as he does, delivery the treat quickly. Repeat for about 10 repetitions, then let him take a break. Repeat the process once more.

Once he is reliably following your lure/hand into a down position, begin labeling his actions. Just as he is starting to lie down, say "down!". Repeat for about 10 repetitions. You should be seeing a pattern of shaping behavior by now. Repetition, labeling, and reward.

SIT AND DOWN: SAY IT ONCE!

You can now "test" him by NOT holding a food lure, but holding your hand as if you are. Ask him to sit. Then slowly and clearly touch the floor as if you had a food lure in your hand and say "down!". Now WAIT! This is important.

If you have his attention and have prepared him so far, he will have some idea of what you are asking of him, but it may take him several seconds or longer to comply. Do NOT repeat your cue. When he does finally lie down, mark and treat.

Teaching the task on cue initially will require a food or toy lure. After several repetitions, try tasks without a lure but be ready to reward quickly when he responds. Moving from lure to reward as quickly as possible will ensure that you do not need to rely on bribery of treats forever.

LURE TO TEACH. REWARD TO REINFORCE

The "touch" cue is next. This will be used later as a focus tool. Like all other behaviors, you are going to capture it. Hold out your hand with your palm facing the puppy. Out of sheer curiosity, he will touch your palm with his nose simply to see what you might have for him. When he does, mark and treat with the other hand. Repeat for 10 repetitions. Let him take a break, then repeat the process. This time around, label his action as "touch!" just as he is touching your hand. Repeat for 10 repetitions, then take a break. While he is a bit distracted, get his attention with his name, hold out your palm, and say "touch!". He should come over to your hand and touch it with his nose. Mark and treat.

Be careful not to "help" him by moving your hand towards his nose! It is very tempting so show him the right answer but remember that he needs to figure it out on his own. Do not reward him if he does not fully touch your palm. Puppies start to learn how to cheat and will possibly lean in the direction of your hand, but not actually touch it. No touch, no reward.

You can begin making it a bit more fun and a bit more difficult by moving your hand into different positions, making sure that he can reach it. Ultimately you want him to move to wherever your hand is to touch it. This will come in handy when you begin working with lots of distractions.

Another great focus tool that you can put on cue is "watch me!" And again, you will begin by capturing the behavior when you see it.

Play a deliberate game of eye contact. Simply sit with your puppy. Every time he makes eye contact with you, mark and treat. Remember that you are not luring him or coaxing him to look at you. Just wait for it to happen. Instill in him that looking at you is very rewarding. Offer him praise and affection, as well. Acknowledging eye contact and rewarding it will help him develop focus as he develops.

Once you have captured and rewarded this behavior over a few days or so, now you can begin labeling the behavior as "watch me!" Give the verbal cue just as your eyes connect. After several repetitions, let him take a break and get distracted a bit. Then get his attention back and say, "watch me!" He should look up at you. When he does, mark and treat.

It can be helpful to add a hand signal. Hold a treat in your hand and put it right to the end of his nose but don't let him take it. Slowly raise the treat/hand up next to your eye level, right at your temple. He will watch the treat as it goes up near your eyes. Watch his eyes carefully and wait for his focus to shift from the treat/hand to your eyes. When it does, mark and treat.

Week 11

Your puppy is showing more confidence this week and should be regularly volunteering good manners. His recall should be the best game ever! He is ready for even more stimulating interactions and novelties.

Meeting Older Dogs

One of the best novelties you can offer your puppy is interactions with older, wiser, mature, patient dogs. It is worth your time and effort to recruit family or friends who may be able to accommodate your puppy. Be sure that the older dog is somewhat familiar with puppies and is patient with them. The goal is to have a positive, or eve neutral, encounter. Never let your puppy meet a dog who may harm him or overwhelm him. In fact, it would be better to skip this exercise rather than risk an encounter that could go poorly.

Once you find the ideal Nanny dog, introduce them in the puppy's home. Try to stay out of the interaction as much as possible initially. Remember that extinction burst? You may see it again here. There is no need to worry or intervene as long as the older dog is trustworthy. Most likely, the older dog will understand that the puppy is uncomfortable and will go about his business, ignoring him until he feels better. Resist the urge to comfort or coddle the puppy! This falls under the category of using stressors. You must allow the puppy to work out how he is feeling and to take his time to assess the situation. His response is normal and hard-wired into his survival instincts.

Not every puppy will be fearful or careful around older dogs. If your puppy is especially boisterous, you will need to guide him as to appropriate ways of interacting with other dogs. Watch the reaction of the older dog. If he is clearly telling the puppy that his play is too rough or obnoxious, call the puppy away from the dog and offer him a toy as a redirection. He needs to learn how to back off and stop his energy when another dog asks him to. If he is especially rough or has too much energy, only allow him brief interactions with the older dog, allowing sniffs and some play bows. Then redirect him again with toys and playtime with you.

If you have older dogs in the home already, they have been interacting with each other already. This is the time to shape that playtime behavior in both dogs.

Decide what level of energy and activity you are comfortable with in your home. Ideally, dogs should not be allowed to wrestle, bite, or otherwise play like "bears" together. Playtime can, and should, be controlled and shaped. Encourage and redirect the play onto tug toys and games of chase. Dogs love to play keep away with each other and it is a great redirection from wrestling. If you feel uncomfortable with the energy level at any point, end the play by separating them.

Game Time!

Just like children, puppies learn best through play. Introducing learning games will keep your puppy engaged and willing to learn. And it's simply fun for you both!

Tug

This is an excellent way to play with your puppy. It is very much a gross motor activity that uses his entire body in a small amount of space. Make the game productive by adding some "rules". That way, he is actually learning as he plays.

The first "rule" is that YOU control the game. Purchase one or two specific tug toys that you will only use for your tug game with him. He may not have access to them outside of your playtime with him. Bring the toy out and wait for him to show you his manners. When he does, invite and entice him to play tug with you. Play as vigorously as you like without letting him get overly excited. After a few minutes, stop your energy and just hold your end of the toy. Disengage from him. He will still be tugging, and it may take him a while to figure out that you have stopped. That's ok. Just wait calmly and quietly. When he stops tugging and eventually lets go of the toy out of confusion, mark and treat him. You have captured the behavior of using his "off switch". It won't last long, however, so once you treat him for stopping the play, immediately begin the game again. His reward for taking a little break is that he gets to continue playing.

Fetch

Most dogs love to chase things that move. Teaching a puppy to fetch relies on his prey drive and willingness to chase after a moving object. If you have a breed with these traits, fetch can be a great outlet.

First, remember that the game is for the dog, not necessarily for you! If he does not learn the game right away or decides that he does not want to bring the toy back to you, it's ok! You are simply introducing a fun game to him at this point. There are no rules. As with all things in this method, patience will pay off.

Start simply by tossing a ball or toy just a foot or 2 away. It's best to pick up other toys to avoid too many distractions. Make sure that he sees the ball move as you toss it. Encourage him with energy and excitement to "get it!" When he does, let him have it as long as he wants it. When he does let go, repeat the game. Do not expect him to bring it back to you yet. Just play a very condensed game of preschool chase.

Drop It!

Not only will your puppy chase toys that you toss, but he is also most likely picking up and carrying things that don't belong to him, too! He is figuring out his boundaries and he needs your guidance. Teaching him to willingly drop or give up an item will help him with those boundaries and can keep him safe.

Engage him in a game of tug. When he releases the toy, even on accident, label that action "Drop!" and reward with a treat.

After rewarding him with the treat, give him the toy back and resume playtime. You are proving to him that good things happen when he volunteers to give up an item. This also prevent confrontations, which is very important for avoiding any form or resource guarding. Yes, you are bigger and stronger than your puppy and can easily pry his mouth open and forcefully remove an item. But all you would prove to your puppy by doing that is that you are a bully and you cannot be trusted. He will be more likely to avoid you when he has found a "treasure" that he is not willing to give up. For his safety and the quality of your communication with him, it is vital that you show him that "sharing" a treasured item is a positive and rewarding behavior.

Hide And Seek

This is one of the best games you can play with your puppy in terms of building a bond. It will help with recall and even leash skills.

It's very simple to introduce. With your puppy watching you, step around a corner or duck behind a couch. Peek out at him briefly so he knows where you are. Do not call or coax him in any way. When he finally "finds you", and he will, reward him with lots of affection and energy and even treats if you like.

As he matures and gains more focus and stamina for games, you can hide in more difficult places. But always remember that is it YOU who hides, not the puppy!

As with everything in Pono Puppy Method, keep your game time short, productive, and positive. There should be no corrections or frustration. Remember that there are no rules, therefore he cannot fail.

SKILLS CHART

Track your progress and stay on track.

+ Proficient! 80% success rate. Keep it up and add a bit of difficulty soon.

✓ Making progress. 50% success rate. Make it a bit easier, keep practice sessions short, reward generously.

— Still learning. Less than 50% success rate. Make it easier, add more short training sessions daily.

	MON	TUES	WED	THURS	FRI	SAT	SUN
LEAVE IT							
RECALL							
CHASE ME							
WATCH ME							
TOUCH							
TUG							
DROP IT							

Puppy Handling and Grooming

It is important to teach your puppy how to be handled and groomed without struggle or conflict. It is not only valuable for daily handling, but it also helps immensely with vet and groomer visits. It is also a precursor to teaching him an "off switch".

Start by sitting on the floor with the puppy sitting between your legs, facing away from you. This is easiest to introduce when he is already a bit tired and more likely to appreciate being still and calm. Hold him gently but firmly by the collar. He will most likely try to turn his head to put his mouth on your hands and may even struggle a bit. Ignore this normal reaction. As you hold his collar with one hand, begin slowly and gently touching his head, face, ears, and mouth. This is a completely non-verbal ritual. Avoid any sort of correction or punishment. This is a form of using a stressor so remain consistent and calm. The stressor is the simple fact that he cannot leave, and it is not playtime. He will be a bit confused until he figures out that this is a calm, peaceful, relaxing interaction between you two.

Work your way down his neck, front legs, back, belly, and hind legs. Maintain a very gentle, relaxing touch and remain silent. You can even play some soothing music if you like. Touch all his feet, spreading the toes and touching the nails. If he struggles or pulls away, just hold firmly and wait for him to settle down again. End your session by laying him on his side (not his back) on the floor and gently holding him in that position until you feel his body relax. This is not a forceful or alpha roll! You are simply asking him to voluntarily lie on his side for just a second or 2. Once he is relaxed, release your gentle hold on him and silently allow him to get up.

HUMAN TOUCH= RELAXATION, NOT CONFRONTATION

The goal of puppy handling is that he learns how to keep himself relaxed and calm during handling. While puppies can easily be manipulated and forced into submission during vet visits and grooming, it is so much better for his brain and well-being for him to learn to volunteer a relaxed, accepting attitude.

Another very important lesson he will learn is the ability to use his "off switch". This falls under the category of impulse control and you will need it to prevent him from becoming unruly and obnoxious as he goes through his adolescent phase.

After a few days of successful puppy handling sessions, start introducing the process during play time. Start a game of fetch or tug and allow him to get mildly excited and engaged. After a few minutes, take the toy away and call him over. Begin your puppy handling session. It will take him a while, potentially, to settle down since he was just in play mode. But muscle memory should kick in and he will remember that this ritual signal calm and relaxation. Keep the "off switch" sessions brief, just a minute or so, so he can be successful. He does not have to fall asleep; he simply needs to give in to your handling calmly. His reward for calming down is that he gets to resume playtime with you. Repeat this one more time.

Several times throughout the day, pick up your puppy and wait for him to completely relax. When he does, immediately put him down and go about your business. You are reinforcing that human touch equals relaxation and it pays off.

Week 12

Your puppy's brain is ready to learn more impulse control. He may be getting more curious and adventurous around the house, even taking things and running off! The sweet, innocence of young puppyhood is disappearing, and he will need to use more self-control and accept more boundaries. You will begin teaching him cues and hand signals that correspond to the behaviors he is already volunteering.

Impulse Control

Last week you began working on puppy handling as an introduction to the "off switch", the first form of impulse control. Now you will start applying that skill to everyday situations, helping him to volunteer more advanced communication skills in order to earn what he wants.

Wait

The feeding ritual, which you began previously, can be expanded to a more difficult task of "wait". Since he is already volunteering to wait for his meals by remaining in a sit position until released to eat, he should translate that skill easily. When you taught the feeding ritual, it was non-verbal. Now, we will begin adding a verbal cue for effective two-way communication.

Start by tempting your puppy with a treat, as you did when you introduced "volunteering manners". He should sit as a natural response by now. When he does, hold up your index finger as a hand signal, and tell him "wait". Attempt to set the treat on the floor a couple of feet away from him, just as you did with the food dish. If he gets up, take up the treat. Repeat as necessary until you can set the treat down without him getting up. When you can, release him to get it. This difference between this and the feeding ritual is that now you are giving a verbal cue and a hand signal. As you repeat the process, he will begin to learn the vocabulary of "wait".

Place Training

Once your puppy begins to understand the concept of waiting, he is ready to begin place training. This is a wonderful tool as it helps him remain, and settle, in one place outside of his pen or crate.

You will need a bed, mat, or raised bed as his "place". It is best to use a unique bed so that he associates it with remaining in place. Avoid using his bed from his crate or pen.

You will begin this training by using capturing. Simply wait for him to investigate the new bed, then mark and treat just like you have been doing for volunteering manners. Remember that he does not have to play your game, but if he does, he will be rewarded! Practice in short sessions and be sure to pick up the bed and keep out of his reach until you are ready to play again.

It will take some practice for him to understand that just staying on the bed gets him treats. If he gets up, and he will, you can step closer to the bed or mat to entice him to get back on it. But remember not to tell him or coax him. The cue will come later.

As he shows more understanding of the game, he will stay on the bed more and wander around less. Now you should start moving around the room a bit. He will get distracted by your movements and will want to come to you for the treat. This is a good way to show him what doesn't work! He will try to figure out if there is another way to get the treat. But there is only one way; stay on the bed. Remember that the key to capturing behaviors is patience. Mistakes are great since they rule out the wrong answers. Let him make mistakes but be ready to reward him when he succeeds.

Track Your Progress

80% Success Rate

☑ **Needs Work: What to Do**

Volunteering Manners

You have most likely rewarded him for being demanding by touching or giving in to him. Be mindful of your response to his actions. Only reward him when he uses his manners.

Recall- Comes When Called

Be sure to play the recall game often! Keep it fun and rewarding. Recall is always accompanied by a high value treat.

Settles in Crate and Pen

Be sure that all his basic needs are met, and he is ready to be calm. Never give him attention or even correction when he is fussing. Experiment with the placement of the crate. Some puppies need to be able to see and hear you while others need to be secluded, dark, and quiet.

Calm For Handling

Consistency and the tenacity on your part to follow through, despite any potential tantrums. This is non-verbal. Resist the urge to try to soothe him verbally. Never scold him for fussing or wiggling. Let him go once he is calm and relaxed.

Waits for Meals Voluntarily

Be sure to control the food. If he gets up before you release him, take the food back up. Repeat as many times as necessary. Never let him approach the food until you have released him to do so.

Waits for a Treat On Cue

Be sure that he is truly waiting before you release him. Ideally, you want eye contact before you let him go get the treat. Be sure to control the treat so he doesn't beat you to it and get inadvertently rewarded!

Allows Trades for Items

Be sure you are not creating confrontation by forcefully taking things from him. If he gets into a guarding state of mind, you may have to loosen him up a bit with redirection. Get him in a playful mood by using your energy and voice. Recall works well here. When he is loosened up, offer a high value treat in exchange for the item you need to take from him.

Redirects onto a Toy When Mouthy

He may be too stimulated. Try a time-out with a boredom buster in the crate or give him some alone time to play in his pen. Make yourself unavailable to him when he is too mouthy.

Responds to Leave It

Practice often so you can be deliberate with your control of the situation and reward. Avoid using it under very distracting environments for now.

Stealing Items

Until your puppy learns that not everything is his to play with, he will make mistakes. You can be guaranteed that he will find something that is either not good for him, or that you simply do not want him to have. Worse yet, he will undoubtedly run off with it!

Check yourself when this happens. Remember, it is not wrong, it is just not good for him. Your first instinct will be to go after him and take it away. Resist this urge, as difficult as it may be. NEVER CHASE A PUPPY! If you chase him, he will run more. And now you have added even more value to the item since you want it too! It will become a game that he controls, and you will not win. Instead, use the tools you already have. Recall is a fantastic way to trick your puppy into forgetting about the new "treasure" he has found. If his recall is good, he will either drop the item to come to you or he will bring it with him when he comes to you. Either way, you have saved him from the item and the item from him.

SOMETIMES YOU HAVE TO GET TRICKY! WHEN ALL ELSE FAILS, DO WHATEVER IT TAKES TO ACCOMPLISH YOUR GOAL. PUPPIES ARE VERY TRAINABLE, BUT NOT ALWAYS VERY SMART. YOU CAN ALWAYS OUTSMART YOUR PUPPY!

There are certainly exceptions where recall simply won't work. Either the item is too much fun, or his recall is not yet strong enough to trump the value of the new treasure. This is when you get creative. Using lots of energy and a fun tone of voice, trick him into thinking that you are doing something much more exciting than he is! Try adjusting your body so you are down lower (puppies can't resist a human who is on their level), find a toy that makes noise, or even shake the treat bag! Anything that accomplishes your goal of getting the forbidden item away from him is valid. The only rule is that you avoid confrontation and punishment. Keep your cool and know that while your puppy is highly trainable, he is not very smart! You WILL be able to trick him into giving up that item, one way or another.

Week 13

Your puppy is growing and learning quickly! While you have had many successes, there are always frustrations and setbacks. Now is the time to go back and do a bit of a refresher. Revisit your checklists and skills charts. Make sure you are keeping up on all your skills so far and insisting constantly on good manners.

The best thing you can do is remain consistent, patient, and gentle with him. Good teachers and leaders understand that if their students are not learning, then the teaching method must be changed. Examine your approach. Check your attitude, timing, and expectations. You may be asking too much of him or not taking enough time to let him figure out what you want from him.

The following pages contain some scenarios that many puppy owners encounter. Some may apply to you. In each case, it is never the puppy's fault. It is not your fault, either necessarily. It is most likely a lack of communication and understanding. Behaviorism is more of an art than a science. Make adjustments to your approach to suit your puppy's temperament and personality type.

What if...

...you lure your puppy into a down position, but he stands up instead?

Ask your puppy to sit and begin again. Each time he stands up, put him back into a sit.

...you hold a treat out and ask for a "sit", but puppy jumps up and bites your hand?

Raise your hand higher and out of his reach for a moment and begin again. Repeat as needed until he settles down.

...you call your puppy, and he does not come?

Be sure you have his attention, and you are being fun and engaging. You can try "tricking" him by squatting down and pretending to "dig" at something on the ground. Curiosity will make him investigate. Reward when he comes.

...your puppy steals a shoe and runs off with it?

Use recall to entice him to come to you. Never scold or yell or chase! If recall does not work, try squeaking a toy or rattling a treat jar. The goal is to retrieve the shoe. Work on "leave it".

...your puppy is still very mouthy and gets really amped up during play time?

Avoid playing rough. Keep your playtime short and keep him out of frenzy mode. Redirect his mouthiness onto toys consistently. Stop all play if he cannot stop biting.

...your puppy nips and jumps while playing the "chase me" game?

Be ready to reward him down low at his nose level. If you hold the treat or toy too high, he will be tempted to jump up to get it. Keep sessions short so he does not get too riled up. This is a game to encourage good recall, not for rough or energetic play.

...your puppy still has trouble settling down in the crate?

Most likely you never got through the extinction burst. If you give up and give in to fussing and crying, he will not settle. Start over and be prepared for noise.

...your puppy does not respond well to recall?

Be sure you are rewarding with a high value treat. If he is not food motivated, play recall games at mealtime. Use toys and playtime as rewards if food does not work. Be sure he is on a leash or long line at all times so he cannot fail.

...your puppy will not wait for meals and gets up without being released?

Be patient and never release him to eat until he has waited without getting up too soon. Good enough is not acceptable.

...your puppy shows fear towards strangers in your home?

Never force him to meet or be held by strangers. Let him approach at his own pace. Leash him so he cannot avoid the person and let them toss treats to him. Make a point of bringing in more people to your home over the next few weeks.

...your puppy is not food motivated?

Find your puppy's currency. If he has a favorite type of toy, try rewarding and luring with it. If your puppy craves attention and affection, use it generously when rewarding.

The Off Switch

Yes, there is a way to shut your puppy off! You began introducing the process with your puppy handling and randomly picking him up and holding him until he settles. Advancing this skill is imperative at this stage.

You have already found that your puppy has certain times of the day when he is amped up. He may have the zoomies, get vocal, attack his toys or even you, and may get very naughty! Managing his energy levels by incorporating use of his "off switch" will help the entire household keep the peace.

Be deliberate and avoid trying to find his "off switch" in the heat of the moment. You will use capturing once again to reward him for calming down and shutting down his energy.

Begin by engaging in a fun, high energy game like tug, fetch, or even recall if he loves to run back and forth between family members as you play your recall game. Just before you think his energy level is going to amp up, shut him down by disengaging and taking the toy or game away. Change your energy and body language to dull and uninteresting. Ignore his attempts to re-engage you. When he finally gives up, resume the play.

Repeat this process several times, making sure that he is truly shutting down in between rounds of play. Avoid letting him get too amped up or it will be harder for him to control his energy level. After the 4th or 5th round of the "off switch" game, end the play altogether and offer him a yummy chew toy or loaded treat toy. If he can't fully settle with a chew toy, put him in his pen or crate.

MODEL
THE
ENERGY
YOU
EXPECT

While it is perfectly normal for a puppy to have bouts of excitement and energy, it is not always good for him, especially in terms of learning good house manners. Being amped up is a difficult state of mind for a puppy to remain in. Your job in everything Pono Puppy is to teach him boundaries, shape his behaviors, and help him live up to your expectations. Teaching him when enough is enough is vital to maintaining balance in the home.

DAILY REMINDERS THIS WEEK

Track your progress daily. Make notes of weak points.

	MON	TUES	WED	THURS	FRI	SAT	SUN
CRATE FOR NAPS AND OVERNIGHT							
RECALL FOR STEALING ITEMS							
SETTLING WHEN HELD							
VOLUNTEERING MANNERS							
PLACE TRAINING PRACTICE							
RECALL EVERY HOUR							
PUPPY HANDLING FOR GROOMING AND NAIL TRIMS*							

*not necessary to trim puppy's nails daily. Practice holding him and touching the feet and nails. If using a Dremel tool, lightly touch each toenail daily.

Week 14

Over the next few months, your puppy will become more independent and curious. This may look a lot like disobedience and defiance, but it is most certainly not. It is a normal part of puppy development. Understanding how to respond to this phase will make life better for everyone.

Wants Vs. Needs

Until recently, most of your puppy's behaviors have reflected his needs. He would get fussy or bossy if he was tired, too hot, too cold, hungry, bored, etc. As he matures, he is discovering that there are things in life that are simply fun and rewarding like playtime, your attention, your affection, treats, and interactions with new things in the world. Some of his behaviors will start reflecting his desires and wants. It may become harder to figure out what he is trying to tell you.

Deciphering what he is asking is mostly a process of elimination. If his basic needs have been met, then demanding behaviors are most likely a result of boredom or under stimulation. This is another learning opportunity for puppy. Not only have you been shaping his behavior to get things he needs, but now you can make him "work" for the things he simply wants.

You do not always have to give the puppy what he wants, however. Sometimes the "want" might be inappropriate at that moment, like wanting to play ball while you are having your dinner. Withholding the "want" until the timing is better gives him a chance to practice some impulse control and think about something else for a while. You will need to offer him a distraction to take his mind off of it. Other "wants" may include things that aren't necessarily good for him like wanting to chase a car. But if the "want" is perfectly appropriate, feel free to give in once you have made sure that he is using his manners.

This phase of development opens the door for learning how to "work" for things. Dogs are happier and healthier when they have a purpose, just like humans. Domesticated dogs do very little in terms of "working" in our culture. Therefore, we must contrive ways to help him feel that he is contributing and earning his resources. Using his "wants" as rewards for responding to basic commands or volunteering good manners helps build intrinsic motivation.

The "work" your puppy will do depends on the basic skills he has so far. Volunteering manners is always appropriate "work". If he has more obedience commands in his skill set, you can ask for a "sit", "down", "shake a paw", or any task he knows. Be consistent with requiring him to "work" for things. Getting everything for free is counterproductive to everything you have worked so hard for in Pono Puppy Method. You run the risk of creating a very spoiled, bossy dog if you constantly cater to his every desire without the requirement of work on his part. You will avoid spoiled puppy syndrome simply by remembering to insist that he earns his keep in the family.

Advanced "Wait"

By now, your puppy should have a good understanding of "wait". You should be able to ask him to sit in one spot as you take several steps away from him and side to side. Now it's time to make it more difficult by adding the Three D's.

The 3 things that make the impulse control tasks more difficult are:

- **DISTANCE**
- **DURATION**
- **DISTRACTION**

The further you get from the puppy, the harder it is for him to stay put. The longer you ask him to sit there and wait, the harder it is for him to be patient. The more distractions going on in the environment, the harder it will be for him to stay focused on his task of not moving.

Teaching a puppy to do nothing is much harder than teaching him to do something. Puppies get easily distracted and bored. Focus skills develop as he matures, so give it time. Increase the difficulty of the "wait" task a little each day, adding a bit more of the 3 D's as you go.

3 D's Worksheet for WAIT

Each day this week, spend a few minutes deliberately strengthening your puppy's "wait" skills. Use the chart to record how far you can move away, how long, and what distractions you added. Refer back to the chart in the future as a reference of progress.

Day	Distance	Duration	Distraction
Monday			
Tuesday			
Wednesday			
Thursday			
Friday			
Saturday			
Sunday			

Impulse control, Off Switch, and Time-Outs

You introduced the "off switch" earlier by playing games of tug and ending the play by stopping your energy and disengaging from him. There will be times when this simply won't be enough to help him settle down and truly shut off. Since he is in a "wants" phase, it may be harder for him to give up on a "want" like fetch and calm himself down.

If his basic needs have been met including exercise and mental stimulation, it is perfectly appropriate to help him settle down by crating him. By now he should definitely associate the crate with peace and quiet. Calmly and positively putting him in his crate will cue him to calm down and take a break. This can be very helpful not only to the humans, but also in helping him practice self-soothing and impulse control.

Another option for a time-out is using place training which you introduced previously. Until now, you have just captured him going to the place and rewarded him. Now, advance your place training work to include cuing him to go to his place. Stand next to the bed. Point to it and use a verbal cue like "Place!". Reward him with a treat when he complies. If he gets up, send him back and treat. Repeat the corrections and send him back to the place every time he gets up. Keep it simple initially and build up his endurance over the next few months. Refer back to the 3 D's; don't go too far from him, don't ask him to stay there too long, and be sure the household is not too busy or distracting. You can offer him a chew bone or other toy to occupy himself as he lies there.

Week 15

Your puppy has grown by leaps and bounds, both physically and mentally. It can be difficult to keep up with such quick changes. In another week or so, the changes will slow down a bit. Of course, he will continue to grow and mature, by the changes will be less abrupt and more predictable, especially if you keep up on Pono Puppy Method.

If you plan to join a puppy kindergarten or other group training program, now is the time to begin doing your research. Find a reputable trainer with plenty of experience with puppies. Keep your expectations realistic. The goal of any group program is to build communication and focus between you and your puppy in the midst of distractions. It will be difficult for him initially. Be prepared to use yummy food treats, a fun toy, and lots of engaging energy to regain his focus when he gets too excited about the environment.

If your puppy is on the shy side, keep your distance from other dogs until he gets more curious and comfortable. Refer back to the stress signals page and watch for signs that he is fearful and when he is trying to cope with this new situation. All of your hard work up until now has helped to prepare him for the next stage of development and for his social journey ahead.

Advancing Leash Work

So far, you have worked on leash skills by capturing the correct behavior of walking next to you or near your space and rewarding it. He is ready for you to show him more boundaries and rules for how to effectively walk with you on a leash.

Choose which side you prefer your puppy to walk on and don't let him change sides as you go. This will be a change for him, and it will be messy for a while. Carefully use your leg closest to him to bump or block him from crossing in front of you. If he tries to cross behind you, use the leash to guide him back to the correct side. The goal is to use the leash as little as possible. Instead, ask yourself how would you get the puppy to walk with you if you didn't have a leash?

The leash is not a steering wheel or brake pedal. Dogs do not come with leashes. This is a very human invention, and it is your job to help the puppy adapt to being tethered to you. If you have been successful and consistent with this program thus far, this transition will be smoother. Think of leash walking as a mini game of "chase me" where he can't get more than the length of leash away from you.

Instead of using the leash to manipulate the puppy, use your voice, energy, body movements, and even toys and treats to help him stay engaged and next to you. If he is pulling ahead, stop and go the other way, coaxing and engaging him at the same time. If he goes left, you go right. Keep your movements random and unpredictable so he has to pay attention. Avoid straight lines. The more you change directions and pace, them more focus he will need to figure out where you are going next. Remember that one of the 3D's is DISTRACTION. That will affect your leash training immensely. He will be very interested in all the smells and exciting things in the world. Your job is to be more engaging and rewarding than the environment.

Keep your leash sessions short and productive. Puppies get tired quickly. If you try to go too far or ask too much of him, he will fail. Several short leash sessions a day are more effective that one or two long walks where he pays no attention to you and is learning to ignore you and pull against the leash. His endurance will develop along with his ability to focus, and you will be able to take longer, productive walks very soon.

BEFORE USING THE LEASH, USE:

**VOICE
ENERGY
EXCITEMENT
MOVEMENT**

Equipment

There are many choices in terms of leashes, collars, harnesses, and other training tools. It can be overwhelming. Where do you start? First, consider your breed. Smaller dogs, under 20 pounds, do quite well in a padded harness. Very often smaller puppies can slip out of collars, so a harness ensures his safety. Be sure that you still incorporate the leash rules, even in a harness. Small dogs often learn to pull since it really doesn't bother the handler. Insist that your small-breed puppy still learns to use good leash manners.

For medium sized dogs, a flat collar or nylon martingale collar is usually effective. If you have a breed with a smaller head, a martingale collar is recommended since he can't slip out of it if he pulls backwards. Harnesses are not recommended for breeds larger than 25-30 pounds. Harnesses are used for sporting dogs to make pulling easier (think sled dog). There are a number of harnesses which are marketed as "no-pull". While they may help initially, there is no tool on the market that will magically prevent your dog from pulling on the leash. This must be accomplished through consistency and reinforcement of correct leash manners.

For large and giant breeds, a head collar is a fantastic option. It works with the same physics as a horse halter. Horses are not led by the neck on a collar and are certainly not lead by a harness. In fact, draft horses are equipped with a harness for pulling wagons. The same reasoning can be applied to large dogs. Since you understand and accept the fact that dogs can, and will, pull against the leash at times, using a tool that gives you a bit gentler control is essential.

The flat collar, martingale, and harness are relatively easy to introduce to your puppy. The head collar will take more conditioning. Most brands come with instructions and tips on how to put it on your puppy as well as how to help him accept it as a positive tool.

A variety of leashes can be helpful for different situations. A regular nylon or cotton 5-foot leash is a great multi-functional tool. You can give him enough room to sniff around at times while not letting him get too far away. A retractable leash is great for hikes and parks where you can let him wander a bit further away. This is a great tool for preparing him for off-leash time since you can practice recall from a greater distance while keeping him safe on the leash.

Remember that no matter what tools you use, communication is first priority.
- VOICE
- ENERGY
- EXCITEMENT
- MOVEMENT

Continue to play the "chase me" game along with recall daily off-leash in your home and yard. The more grounded he is with these games, the easier the transition to leash work will be.

Balance

As your puppy's endurance grows, so will your temptation to do more with him. Carefully consider your puppy's breed, temperament, and energy level. It will be tempting to jump right into all the great activities that you have been waiting to do with your pup. Keep your outings and training sessions short. If you do too much, you run the risk of not only putting undo strain on his growing body, but he may begin to resent outings and training sessions. Be patient with his development. If you stick with the activities and lessons in Pono Puppy Method, he will be well-prepared for bigger, longer, and more exciting activities very soon.

Offer your puppy a variety of stimulation throughout the day, just like when he was very young. Some puppies at this stage need even more routine and a stricter schedule. Consider putting him on a schedule like a toddler. Offer him opportunities for enrichment, exercise, brain work in the form of training and/or puzzle toys, and plenty of quiet rest time at regular intervals throughout the day. This is especially important if you are experiencing bossier and demanding-type behaviors. That could be your cue that he is not getting enough balance in his routine.

Week 16

This is an exciting time for you and your puppy! He should be ready for his final set of immunizations and fully equipped with the necessary social skills to venture out into the world! Time to show off your amazing, well-mannered puppy.

Expectations

You have worked very hard over the past 2 months preparing your puppy for his journey ahead. Don't let all those good habits fade. Not only will your puppy be distracted by new things and people in the environment, but so will you. Keep your focus on your puppy and his training. It will be tempting to let everyone pet him. And people WILL want to stop and pet him! After all, he is an adorable puppy.

While it is important for your puppy to meet new people and have positive interactions with them, it can also be counterproductive to his training, especially if he is a very social breed. If he is allowed to greet every new human, you will create that pattern of expectation. He will insist that you stop and say hello to everyone. The key is to decide when and if he will greet. A general rule of thumb is "not every person, not every time."

The same thing applies to meeting other dogs. If you allow him to greet every new dog he sees, it will become problematic later. It is very frustrating when your puppy insists on saying hi to every dog you pass.

The good news is that you can find a balance. You are in control of every situation you and your puppy encounter. Decide ahead of time who he will greet, how he will greet, and when that greeting will end.

If your puppy is especially social and outgoing, it is best to avoid greetings on walks until his focus skills are more developed. It may sound counterintuitive, but this helps the overly social pup learn to have more impulse control. If you find that your puppy is interested in other people or dogs, build more distance and work on his basic obedience skills in a distracting place. As you pass by people, dogs, and other distractions, use a treat or toy to keep his attention on you. Remember the 3D's and adjust them so he can be successful. Work his focus skills until he can focus longer with more distractions. It is a process that comes with maturity so work as slowly as necessary so he can be successful.

NOT EVERY PERSON, NOT EVERY TIME

If your puppy is a bit more reserved and uncertain about new people and dogs, you will need the opposite approach. Give him lots of opportunities to say hello to people and to greet older, quiet dogs. Be sure that you ask the person to come down to his level. It may help to let the stranger offer your puppy a treat. Practice his obedience and focus skills in areas that are moderately distracting, especially around people and other dogs. If he is feeling apprehensive, responding to obedience tasks will help him feel better since it is something he is confident in.

Managing Greetings

GREETING PEOPLE

When it is appropriate to greet someone, establish the rules right away.

- Get your puppy's attention. He should look at you.
- Give the puppy a verbal cue like, "go say hi" that tells him it's ok to greet someone.
- Instruct the person to either bend or squat down to his level if possible.
- Allow the puppy to approach the person on his own. This gives him a voice in the interaction. He gets to decide if he wants to greet that person or not. If he does not approach the person, do not let them pet him. Only allow a greeting if the puppy is actively interested in participating.
- Be sure the leash is short enough to prevent him from jumping up. Hopefully by now he is proficient in offering manners and will keep his feet on the ground. If not, you can prevent jumping by keeping the leash short. If he jumps up, end the greeting and walk away. Once he has settled down, try again. This is important, especially if he does want to greet someone. He will learn that the only way to get affection is to keep his feet on the ground.

ATTENTION.
CUE.
CONTROL
LEASH.
KEEP IT
BRIEF.

GREETING DOGS

Greeting new dogs requires rules, as well.

- Get his attention, especially when he has already seen the other dog and is getting distracted. If you cannot get his attention, walk away and build distance. This will help him get his focus back onto you.
- Give him a verbal cue like, "go say hi" and allow him to approach. He will most likely pull as he approaches, so be ready to move with him.
- Keep the leash as loose as possible. Avoid adding tension to the greeting.
- Keep the greeting short and positive, about 3-5 seconds. The dogs should sniff each other and show some interest. Never allow playtime while on a leash. This is just a quick greeting to build confidence and satisfy curiosity. Playtime is always off-leash in a safe area.
- Once they have had a quick greeting, give another verbal cue like, "let's go" and walk away. It may take some coaxing and prompting so make yourself fun and energetic. He should happily come away from the other dog and resume his walk with you.

Building Leadership

Taking your puppy on outings is a fabulous opportunity to build your leadership skills with him.

A good leader will communicate effectively, listen attentively, and model behaviors and attitudes clearly.

Take advantage of this special time together out in the world. He is looking to you for guidance and confidence. You are well-equipped to help him explore and be enriched on your field trips. You have learned how to recognize and deal with a fear response and should be able to read his body language clearly by now. Be confident in your handling of him, making all of the decisions along the way.

Decide in advance not only where you will go for your first outing, but the duration, pace, and level of exposure he is ready for. Be sure to not overwhelm him. Your first outing should be someplace that you are very familiar and comfortable with. Think of it as showing him a special part of your world that you would like to share with him. Allow him time and space to scope out this new environment, but avoid letting him call the shots, so to speak. Set the pace of your walk, decide the direction, and invite him to follow along. Introduce him to novel things as you encounter them. He will be interested in gobbling up leaves, sticks, or even rocks if given a chance. As much as possible, keep his mind and focus on other things like "chasing" you, doing short recall, and any obedience commands he is familiar with. Your first outing will not be a free-for-all. In fact, no outing should ever be without boundaries and expectations. He will have plenty of fun and enrichment, especially if you remain in charge. By establishing boundaries in the real world, you are boosting your leadership immensely and he will see you as confident and reliable.

Building Focus

Over the past couple of months, you have seen a good deal of growth in terms of your puppy's attention span and focus skills. This will continue to improve as he matures, though there will be plenty of times when the environment will be challenging for him.

Continue to work on focus skills at home and under very little distraction. Be sure that it is very worthwhile for him to look away from a distraction and back at you. Eye contact is the key. When your puppy can focus on you, he cannot react to the distractions around him. It is simply incompatible. That is the goal. If you insist that your puppy gives you his attention when prompted, you can prevent difficult behaviors from developing.

You have most likely witnessed the dog who is very reactive towards other dogs. That behavior developed because the handler did not understand the importance of focus. They may say that their puppy never pays attention, while the fact is, he is paying very good attention, just not to the handler. Puppies are very aware of their surroundings. How they feel and respond to it is completely within your control.

Remember that Pono Puppy Method relies on capturing behaviors whenever possible. This applies to focus tasks, too. As you encounter a distraction, stop and wait. Stay far enough away that he can experience it without getting too stimulated. Be his anchor. Let him watch. If/when he decides to check in with you by making eye contact, mark and treat. If he cannot stop watching the action and seems too locked in on it, whether it be a dog or children or whatever the distraction is, you may need to build more distance and try again. Whenever he makes the choice to look at you, reward him. You must be watchful and pay attention to him to do this.

FOCUS TASKS

- WATCH ME
- RECALL
- CHASE ME
- BACK PEDALING
- TOUCH
- CAPTURING EYE CONTACT

The reality of walking a puppy in a new place is that it will be messy, exhausting, and will require you to pay close attention to him and how he is responding. Establishing your expectations for how he is to behave on-leash now is paramount. Avoid using his age as an excuse for poor manners and leash skills. Yes, he is young, and this is all new. But he is capable of living up to your expectations, be they high or low. Have patience and keep your outings short, successful, positive, and productive. Remember you are shaping him into the dog he is destined to become.

A Strong Foundation

What an amazing journey you have embarked on! Congratulations on all your hard work and dedication. You should be reaping the rewards of a close relationship with your puppy based on respect, communication, and positivity. But this is just the beginning!

Where to go From Here

First, consider your breed and his strengths. Find activities, games, groups, and program that are designed to meet his instinctive drives. Joining programs or social groups is a great way to meet other people who share your passion for training and enjoyment of their dogs. It can also give you some motivation to and accountability to continue training.

If social outlets aren't of interest to you, there are plenty of other ways to fulfill your puppy's needs and continue his training. Resources are abundant online and in your community. Find what works for you to continue his development. The bottom line is that you have worked hard to build a strong foundation with your puppy. Now he is ready for greater challenges and opportunities. Don't stop! Learning is for life. Your puppy has much more to learn and to improve upon.

A World of Opportunity

Take some time to research and learn about types of classes, games, and programs in your area that pique your interest. Some ideas include:

- Therapy dog work
- Scent and detection work
- Rally and obedience through AKC
- Search and Rescue training
- Agility
- Fly Ball

Discovering a hobby or sport that you both enjoy that will help you continue training with your puppy. Revisit this workbook often to reinforce your foundational work and keep up on manners and basic skills. May you feel confident and prepared with Pono Puppy Methods as you venture ahead.

Made in the USA
Las Vegas, NV
30 January 2024

85043084R00059